Cambridge **Discovery Education**™

▶ **INTERACTIVE READERS**

Series editor: Bob Hastings

SECRETS TO A LONG LIFE

B1

Diane Naughton

CAMBRIDGE
UNIVERSITY PRESS

Discovery
EDUCATION™

CAMBRIDGE UNIVERSITY PRESS
Cambridge, New York, Melbourne, Madrid, Cape Town,
Singapore, São Paulo, Delhi, Mexico City

Cambridge University Press
32 Avenue of the Americas, New York, NY 10013-2473, USA

www.cambridge.org
Information on this title: www.cambridge.org/9781107683785

© Cambridge University Press 2014

First published 2014

Printed in Hong Kong, China, by Golden Cup Printing Company Limited

A catalog record for this publication is available from the British Library.

Library of Congress Cataloging-in-Publication Data

Naughton, Diane.
 Secrets to a long life / Diane Naughton.
     pages cm. -- (Cambridge discovery interactive readers)
 ISBN 978-1-107-68378-5 (pbk. : alk. paper)
 1. Longevity--Juvenile literature. 2. English language--Textbooks for foreign speakers.
 3. Readers (Elementary) I. Title.

RA776.75.N387 2013
613.2--dc23

                                2013018629

ISBN 978-0-521-978-1-107-68378-5

Additional resources for this publication at www.cambridge.org

Layout services, art direction, book design, and photo research: Q2ABillSMITH GROUP
Editorial services: Hyphen S.A.
Audio production: CityVox, New York
Video production: Q2ABillSMITH GROUP

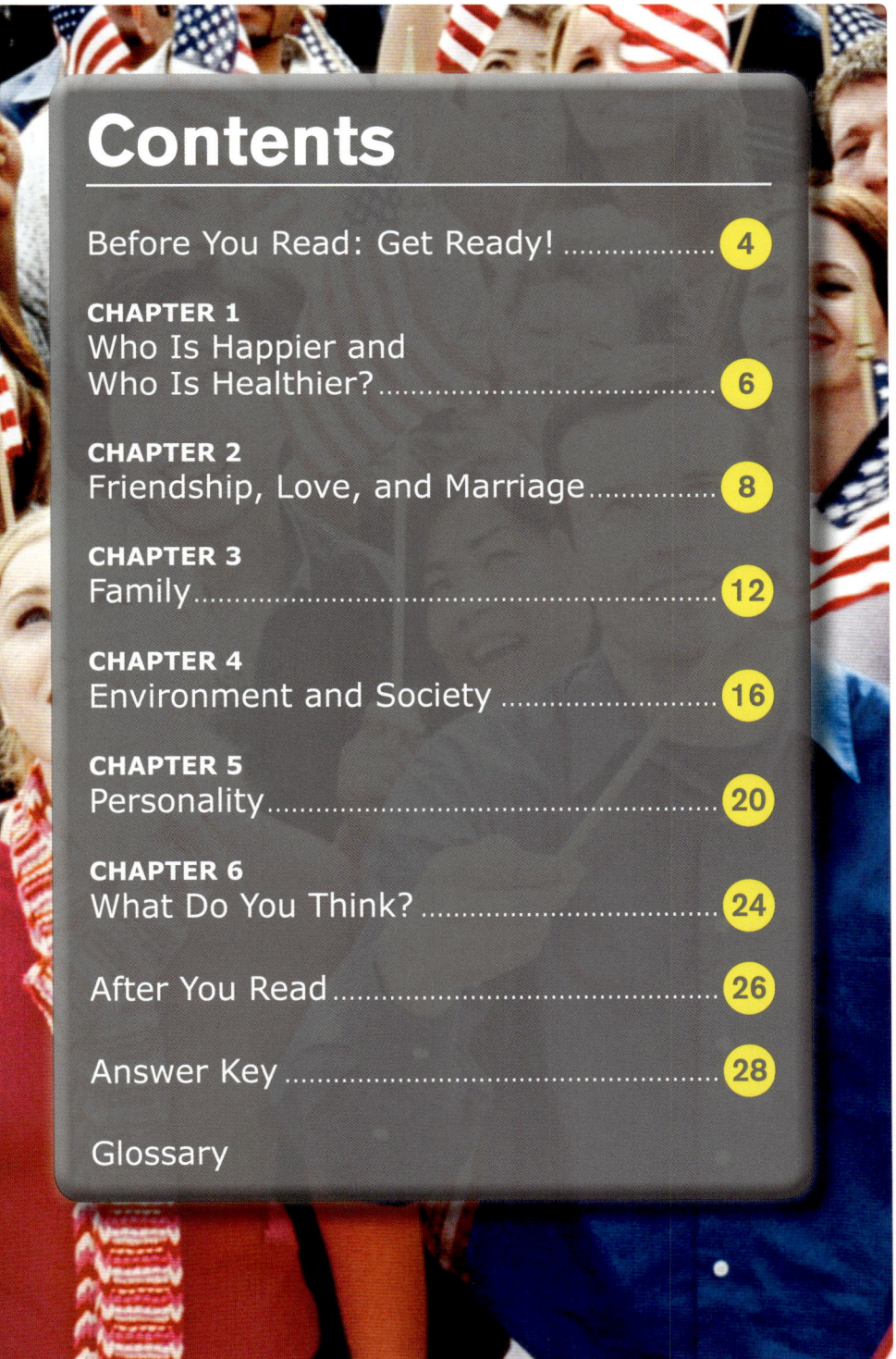

Contents

Before You Read: Get Ready!

Words to Know

Complete the sentences with the correct words.

siblings

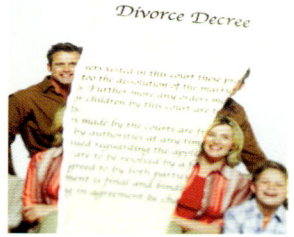
identical twins

divorce

personality

community

1 A _____ is a group of people who live in the same area. They often share some interests.

2 _____ are born to the same mother at the same time. They look the same.

3 _____ is the set of qualities – like adventurous, funny, kind – that describes a person.

4 _____ belong to the same family. They can be brothers or sisters.

5 A _____ is when two people end their marriage.

Read the paragraph. Then complete the definitions with the correct highlighted words.

    In modern society we often have very stressful lives, and this can be bad for our health. Stress can give us physical problems, like headaches or heart problems, and emotional problems, too. Even confident, happy people can start to feel worried or depressed when under stress. When people feel like this, they may benefit from doing exercise because it helps them relax.

1 _____: connected to the body

2 _____: very sad, often for a long time

3 _____: a big group of people who live together in an organized way

4 _____: get something good that helps you

5 _____: connected to the mind and feelings

6 _____: certain about your ability to do things well

?

ANALYZE

This book is about the things that help people have a long and happy life. How important do you think the following things are: friends, love, marriage, siblings, environment, society, personality?

CHAPTER 1

Who Is Happier and Who Is Healthier?

DO YOU KNOW ANY REALLY HAPPY, HEALTHY PEOPLE? WHY ARE THEY LIKE THAT? IS IT MONEY, LOVE, OR ARE THEY JUST LUCKY?

Often on TV or in magazines we see the rich and famous: successful film stars, singers, and sports people. They live in beautiful homes. They drive expensive cars. They even have their own planes. Sometimes we may think, "Wouldn't it be great to be like them!" But how do we know the rich and famous are happy?

Most of us are not famous or rich, and we have to work hard for our money. But sometimes we spend it on things we don't really need: an expensive pair of shoes, the newest mobile phone, or the biggest TV screen. We sometimes even want to change our **physical** appearance; we tell ourselves it would be great to be slimmer or to have younger-looking skin! But do those things really make us happier or healthier?

Of course, money is important. We need it to have a comfortable place to live and to pay the bills. But money isn't everything. If we work too much, we may not have time for family or friends. If we think only about the expensive things we want to buy, we might forget to enjoy simple pleasures, like a walk in the country, a conversation with a good friend, or a simple meal at home. As the song says, "Money can't buy me love!"

We all want to be healthy and happy, but it's difficult to say what the secrets of a long and happy life are. Studies show that many things can be important, and they connect together in different ways. Read on to find out how some people find health and happiness.

EVALUATE

Think of the things that make you happy. Which of them cost a lot of money? Which of them don't? So, how important is money for your happiness?

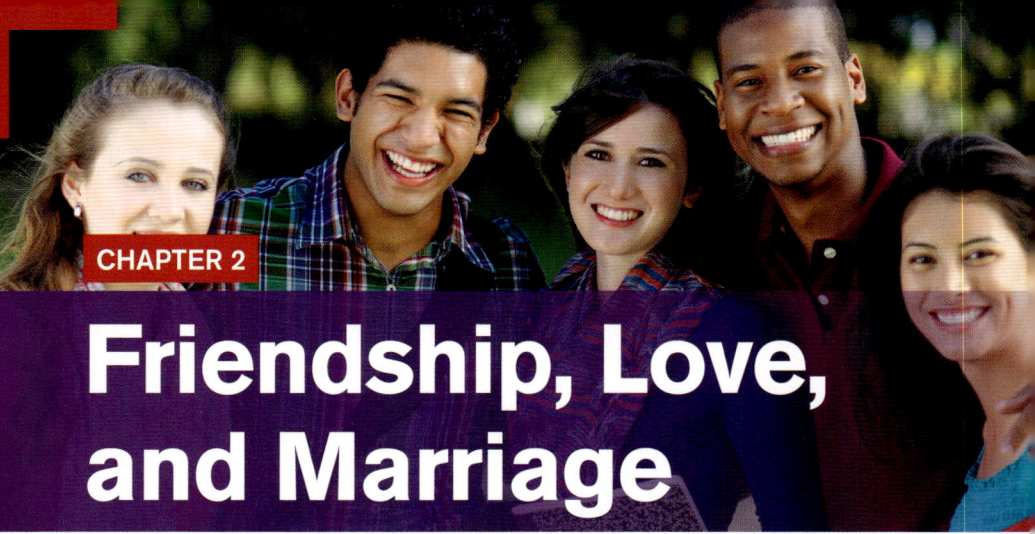

CHAPTER 2

Friendship, Love, and Marriage

DO YOU HAVE A LOT OF FRIENDS? DO YOU GET ON WELL WITH YOUR CLASSMATES, COWORKERS, AND NEIGHBORS? ARE YOU IN LOVE? THE MORE "YES" ANSWERS YOU HAVE TO THESE QUESTIONS, THE HAPPIER YOU PROBABLY ARE!

When we have good relationships with other people, we generally feel better both physically and emotionally. It's not just fun to have friends, we actually need them! They are there to celebrate good things with us, like birthdays or passing exams. But they also help us through the bad times: losing a job, money problems, or the death of someone we love.

In fact, a 2010 study at Brigham Young University in Utah, USA, showed that people with good friends had 50 percent more chance of living longer. They found that not having friends can be as dangerous for our health as smoking 15 cigarettes a day. And being lonely is even more dangerous than not doing physical exercise or being overweight.

So friendship is good for us, but what about falling in love? Helen Fisher of Rutgers University in New Jersey, USA, is an expert on love and attraction. She found that when a person is in love, more blood travels to certain parts of the brain. This means happy chemicals[1] called endorphins are made, and we experience a strong feeling of pleasure. Sometimes we find it impossible to think about anything else but Mr. or Ms. Right. We can't sleep or eat, but we're very happy.

So love actually changes our brains! We stop thinking about "I" and start thinking about "We." When we have a good relationship with our partner, we feel safer, worry less, and learn to enjoy more things. A loving couple can benefit from each other's **strengths** and cover each other's **weaknesses**.

[1]**chemicals:** things in our bodies that affect our emotions

James Coan, a scientist from Virginia University, wanted to see whether feelings of love could help people stay calm and feel less pain. He did an experiment on women who were in a loving relationship.

First, he gave them an electric shock[2] and asked them how much pain and **emotional** stress they felt. Then, he allowed the women to hold hands with their partners while he gave them another shock. Again, he asked them how they felt. This time, they reported that the shock gave them less pain and stress. Studies of the women's brain **activity** also showed that they were calmer before and during the second shock.

So love may keep us calm and make us feel less pain, but be careful. A broken heart can hurt just like an illness can! Scientist Naomi Eisenberger has shown that the part of the brain that is **active** when we feel physical pain is also active when a loved one leaves us.

[2]**electric shock:** a painful feeling you get when you touch electricity

Video Quest

Marriage and Divorce

Watch this video to learn about marriage and divorce rates in the USA. How many people are married? How many marriages end in divorce?

If falling in love makes us happy and healthy, what about marriage? Studies show that married men and women are happier and healthier than single or divorced people. On average, single people are more likely to get ill, spend more time in the hospital, and die younger. They also feel depressed more often and behave in ways that are bad for their health. Single men, for example, drink twice as much alcohol[3] as married men, and 25 percent of them say that this is a problem.

Married people also benefit because two people can live together more cheaply than one person. They share the house, car, food, and bills. Both married men and women seem to do better at work, too. They earn more and get more important jobs. Married men are also more likely to arrive at work on time!

[3] **alcohol:** drinks such as wine and beer

CHAPTER 3

Family

PARTNERS AND CHILDREN APPEAR LATER IN OUR LIVES. PARENTS USUALLY LEAVE US TOO EARLY. BUT BROTHERS AND SISTERS ARE OFTEN WITH US FOR ALMOST ALL OUR LIVES. FOR BETTER OR FOR WORSE!

Bringing up two or more kids under the same roof often means trouble. Siblings take each other's things and fight for their parents' attention. In fact, a recent study in England showed that 31 percent of children were unhappy because a sibling fought with them a lot.

But these fights can be good for us, too. They are an **opportunity** to face problems in an emotionally safe environment. An argument at breakfast is forgotten by lunch. As British poet Dylan Thomas once said, "I made a snowman and my brother knocked it down and I knocked my brother down and then we had tea."

Barack Obama, Ben Affleck, and JK Rowling are all first-born children.

It seems that we benefit especially from having sisters. A study at the University of Ulster in the U.K. found that when we have girls for siblings, honest communication in the family **increases**. This is good for our emotional health.

Now let's think about another family matter! What do Barack Obama, Ben Affleck, and JK Rowling have in common? They're all rich, successful, and first-born children. In fact, more than half of US Presidents and Nobel Prize winners were first-born. A study by the newspaper USA TODAY found that 43 percent of the bosses of large companies were also first-born. Why might this be?

Well, parents usually give more attention to first-born children, and they expect great things from them. As a result, these children are often responsible and confident. They do well at school, and some studies suggest they are more intelligent than their younger siblings. But the first-born can have weaknesses, too. They sometimes expect too much of themselves and try too hard to be perfect. This can make them worry and feel afraid of failing.

Last-born children – the "babies of the family" – usually get a lot of attention, too. They are often loving, **sociable**, and charming. They are freer than their older siblings and more likely to do dangerous or unusual things. They often break the rules, like the Polish scientist Copernicus. He was the youngest of four children. In 1543, he shocked the world when he wrote a book saying that the Earth moves around the Sun. At that time, everybody was sure that the Sun moved around the Earth, and some people were very angry when Copernicus said they were wrong.

What about the poor kids in the middle? Studies say they get less attention and are rarely favorites. But don't worry if you're a middle child. There are some great members in your club! Bill Gates, John F. Kennedy, and Madonna are all middle children.

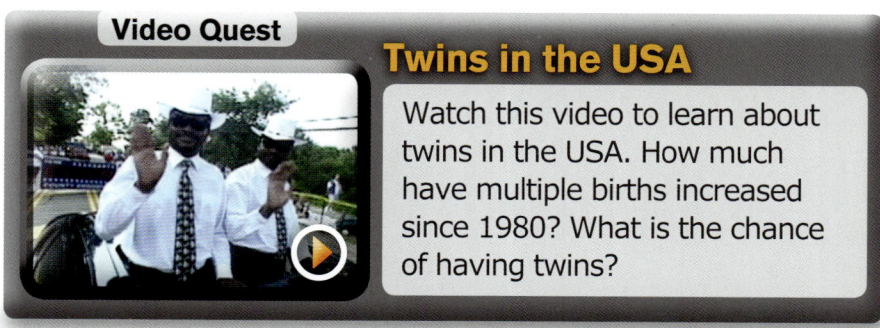

Video Quest

Twins in the USA

Watch this video to learn about twins in the USA. How much have multiple births increased since 1980? What is the chance of having twins?

Is it sad to be brought up as an only child, with no brothers and sisters to play with? In the past, people thought so. But lots of recent studies show that only children are often happy and successful. The actress Natalie Portman once said that her parents allowed her to become an actress because she was an only child. Her parents didn't have to worry about her being seen as "special" or different from any siblings. She didn't steal attention away from anyone. She could be happy doing whatever she wanted.

Lastly, we have the question of multiple[4] births. How does it feel to be a twin? Twins can have extremely close relationships, and this can help them get through life. But sometimes it's difficult for twins to show their own personalities. They have to remind people: "Please, it's not us. It's me!"

[4]**multiple:** many things at the same time

It's hard to breathe when you have asthma.

CHAPTER 4

Environment and Society

WHERE DO HAPPY, HEALTHY PEOPLE LIVE? IN THE CITY OR THE COUNTRY? IN DENMARK OR JAPAN? IN RICH PLACES OR POOR ONES?

People often think that living in the countryside is best. There's clean air, fresh food, and lots of physical activity to do. It's true that nature is good for us. If we spend lots of time outside, we feel less stressed and are less likely to get fat. Children benefit especially and have fewer breathing problems like asthma.[5]

But some studies in the USA show that people in cities live longer and healthier lives. They generally eat better food, do more exercise, and smoke less. They also have more doctors and hospitals. Surprisingly, there are fewer deaths from traffic accidents in cities.

[5] **asthma:** an illness that makes it difficult to breathe

People can drive much faster in the countryside, which is dangerous, and it takes longer to get to a hospital when someone is hurt. City people generally earn more money, so they can take better care of themselves, too. The average salary[6] in US cities is $53,000 compared to $39,000 in country areas.

What kind of city is the best to live in? In 2008, a Gallup[7] study compared ten important international cities, including New York, London, Berlin, and Tokyo. They found that people were happy if their city was beautiful, clean, and safe. It was also important to have good public transportation and lots of places for people to spend their free time, like movie theaters, parks, and sports centers. Other studies have shown that people are happy when their neighborhoods have a strong sense of community, the neighbors are sociable, and they help each other.

....

[6]**salary:** the money you get, usually every week or month, for working

[7]**Gallup:** an American organization that often collects information about society by doing interviews with many people

EVALUATE

Think about the place where you live.
Do you think it's a happy, healthy place?
Why or why not?

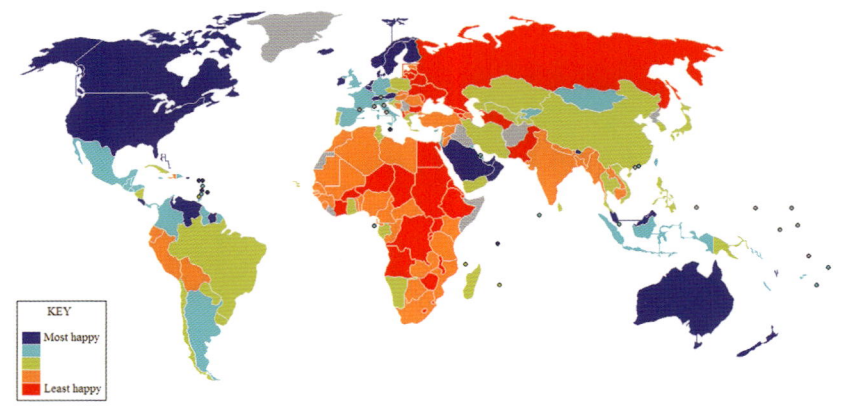

KEY

Most happy

Least happy

Which are the best countries to live in? Adrian White, a British scientist, has made the first world map of happy and unhappy countries.

1	Denmark
2	Switzerland
3	Austria
8	Bhutan
23	USA
41	UK
90	Japan
125	India
167	Russia
178	Burundi

He looked at nearly 200 international studies and put 178 countries in order from the most happy and healthy to the least. Here are some results.

As you can see, Denmark was at the top of the list. Not only does Denmark have a good climate and beautiful landscapes, but in this country, people in full-time jobs work only 37 hours a week. Most people take five weeks of vacation every year. They have free health care and higher education. Although they have to pay as much as 50 percent of their salaries in taxes,[8] they are happy to do this because the money goes back to the community. Almost all adults (95 percent) belong to a club or community organization.

[8]**tax:** money you have to pay to the government

In today's society, many governments think the Gross National Product (GNP)[9] is the best way to show how successful a country is. But in Bhutan, a small Buddhist[10] country in the South Asian Himalayas, people see things differently. In 1972, King Jigme Singye Wangchuck decided that instead of looking at the GNP, he would look at the GNH, or Gross National Happiness. He believed that to see how well a country is doing, we have to look at more than money. We need to think about people's quality of life, free time, and community relationships.

These days, many people think that our stressful way of life is making us unhappy. In 1986, Carlo Petrini started the Slow Movement when he tried to stop a McDonald's restaurant from opening in Rome. People in the Slow Movement believe that modern life is too fast; we must slow down and spend more time with our loved ones.

[9] **Gross National Product (GNP):** the money a country makes in a year
[10] **Buddhist:** connected to the religion of Buddhism

? ANALYZE

Look at the chart of happy and unhappy countries again. Why do you think that Japan, India, or Russia didn't do very well?

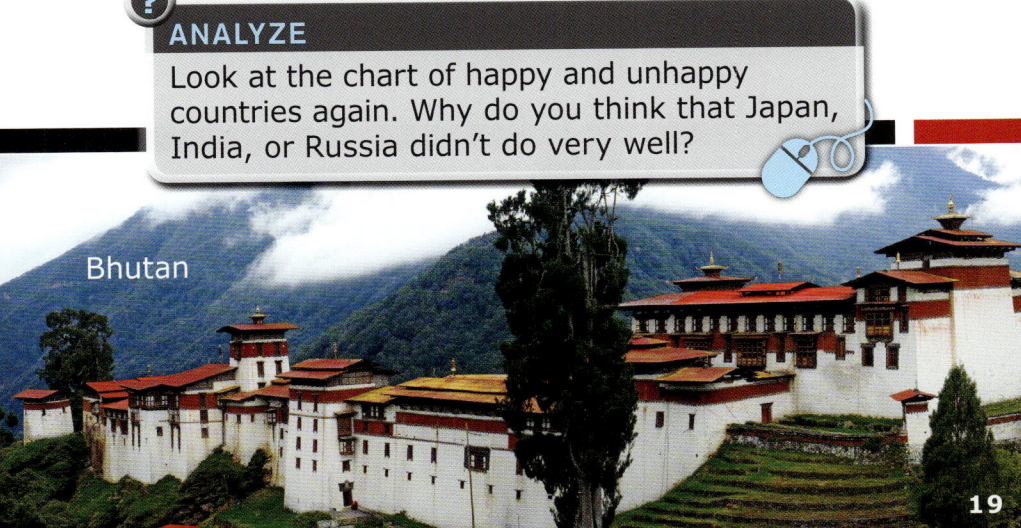

Bhutan

19

Do you see the glass as half full or half empty?

½ full

½ empty

CHAPTER 5

Personality

ARE SOME PEOPLE NATURALLY HAPPIER AND HEALTHIER THAN OTHERS?

When we are born, we already have a kind of photo of our lives inside us. Because of our DNA,[11] we might have more or fewer physical problems than other people. We are also emotionally different from others.

Studies have been done on identical twins that were separated as babies and brought up in different environments. As adults, they still had very similar physical and emotional strengths and weaknesses. Scientists believe that DNA is partly responsible for their personalities. They say that each of us has a kind of natural happiness point. This decides how happy we are likely to be. When bad things happen, we can fall below this point, but we will return to it with time.

[11] **DNA:** the special chemical at the center of all living things that controls what they are like; it makes each thing special and different from others.

So happiness does not depend so much on how many good or bad experiences we have but on how we see those experiences. One person's problem can be another person's opportunity. You may see a glass that is half full, whereas your unhappy friend sees a glass that is half empty.

Think about this question:

You have planned a picnic in the countryside for your birthday. On the morning news, they say it might rain. What do you do?

- Ⓐ Tell your friends there won't be a picnic and stay at home alone feeling depressed.

- Ⓑ Have the picnic in the park near your house. If it rains, you can invite your friends back home.

- Ⓒ Have the picnic in the countryside as planned. It might not rain, and if it does, maybe it will be fun to get wet!

Which answer would make you the happiest? Remember: To be happy and healthy, we have to be confident, cheerful, and hopeful about the future!

In a recent Gallup study, one million Americans were asked about their lives: happiness, work, illnesses, stress, etc. From the results, Alvin Wong, a 65 year-old Chinese-American, was found to be America's happiest man. He is married with children, lives in Hawaii, and has his own business. When talking about the secret of happiness he said, "You don't do things just for money. You do things because you want to do them, you love to do them. This is what's going to make you want to get up in the morning."

Some scientists say that our natural happiness point explains about 50 percent of our feelings. Our life experiences probably explain another 10 percent. But amazingly, about 40 percent of our ability to be happy is within our power to change. Personality is not like eye color. We can change the way we think and behave.

French scientist and writer Matthieu Ricard has been called the world's happiest man after scientific studies were done on his brain activity. He is a Buddhist, and he lives in the Himalayas. He says that happiness is an ability that everyone can learn.

There are two sides to our brains. The left side is connected to feelings of happiness, and the right side is connected to unpleasant emotions. We can learn through meditation[12] to use the left side more often. The idea is to think about experiences that have made us truly happy – on the inside – instead of those short moments of excitement that pass quickly.

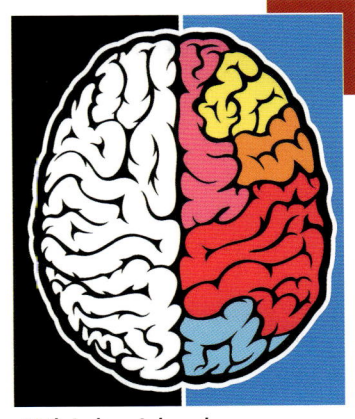

Which side do you think with?

Happier people also live longer. The world's oldest person was Jeanne Calment, who died in 1997 at the age of 122. At 120, she said the secret of her long life was having fun and enjoying nice things.

[12]**meditation:** when you give all your attention to one thought for some time; Buddhists often do it.

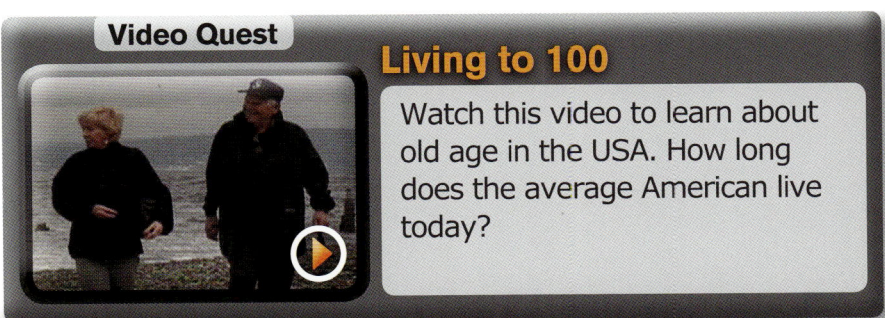

Video Quest

Living to 100

Watch this video to learn about old age in the USA. How long does the average American live today?

CHAPTER 6

What Do You Think?

HOW HAPPY AND HEALTHY ARE YOU?

Answer YES (Y) or NO (N) to these questions.

1. Do you have some good friends that you have fun with and that help you when you have a problem? _____

2. Do you have good relationships with the people you study/work with? _____

3. Are you in a close relationship with one special person who you feel completely safe with? _____

4. Do you get along with your parents / siblings? _____

5. Do you have frequent contact with nature? _____

6. Are you physically active? _____

7. Do you live in a beautiful place? _____

8. Is the place where you live clean and safe? _____

9. Do you belong to any clubs or organizations? _____

10. Are you sociable with your neighbors? _____

11. Do you have enough free time? _____

12. Do you sometimes take life slowly, enjoying what you are doing? _____

13. Do you often have opportunities to do good things? _____

14. Do you love many of the things that you do? _____

15. Are you hopeful about the future? _____

How many YES answers have you got?

Results

10–15: Wow! You are an extremely happy person, and you are likely to have a long life.

6–9: You're not very happy, but you're not terribly sad either. In fact, you are probably quite normal.

0–5: Too bad! You don't seem to be having a great time at the moment. Try making some changes.

Don't worry if your results are bad. You can make things better. If you think happy thoughts, you can be happy.

Try this exercise for a week. Before you go to sleep every night, think of ten good things, big or small, that have happened to you during the day. It may be difficult, but if you try, you will find them. Life may start to look a little sweeter.

After You Read

Choose the Correct Answers

Read the following sentences and choose Ⓐ, Ⓑ, Ⓒ, or Ⓓ.

1 In one experiment, women felt less pain from an electric shock if they _____ .

Ⓐ took strong medicine
Ⓑ held their partner's hand
Ⓒ felt very happy
Ⓓ were young and healthy

2 Family members might talk more to each other if some of the children are _____ .

Ⓐ similar
Ⓑ different
Ⓒ boys
Ⓓ girls

3 The oldest child in a family is more likely to _____ .

Ⓐ be sociable
Ⓑ live dangerously
Ⓒ have success
Ⓓ get married

4 In Denmark, people have to _____ .

Ⓐ give a lot of money to the government
Ⓑ work more than forty hours a week
Ⓒ belong to a community organization
Ⓓ pay for health care and education

5 GNH tells us how _____ .

Ⓐ rich a country is
Ⓑ healthy a country is
Ⓒ successful people are
Ⓓ happy people are

6 We know about the natural happiness point because of experiments on _____ .

(A) close friends
(B) identical twins
(C) Danish people
(D) happy people

Complete the Text

Use the words in the box to complete the paragraph.

| brain   community   exercise   married   opportunity   siblings |

There are many secrets to a long and happy life. Fall in love and get
1 _____ . Make sure you have lots of friends around.
Try to get along well with your **2** _____ ; they can
help you on the journey of life. Do **3** _____ in the
open air and take part in your **4** _____ ; neighbors are
important, too. But most of all, remember to use the left side of your
5 _____ . From a bad experience you might find a
wonderful **6** _____ .

Evaluate

Read the sentences and check (✓) whether you agree.
Then give a reason why or why not.

	Agree?	Reason
Most of the married people I know are happier than the single ones.		
I would like to be an identical twin or an only child.		
I think I can teach myself to be happier.		

Answer Key

Words to Know, page 4

1 community **2** Identical twins **3** Personality
4 Siblings **5** divorce

Words to Know, page 5

1 physical **2** depressed **3** society **4** benefit
5 emotional **6** confident

Analyze, page 5   *Answers will vary.*

Evaluate, page 7   *Answers will vary.*

Video Quest, page 10
More than half of the population over 15 is married. The
chance of a marriage lasting is 57 percent. You can have a
better chance by waiting until you are at least 25 to marry.

Video Quest, page 14
Multiple births have increased by 70 percent since 1980.
The chance of having twins is 3.1 percent or one woman
in 32.

Evaluate, page 17   *Answers will vary.*

Analyze, page 19   *Answers will vary.*

Video Quest, page 23
The average American lives to be 79.

Choose the Correct Answers, page 26
1 B **2** D **3** C **4** A **5** D **6** B

Text Completion, page 27
1 married **2** siblings **3** exercise **4** community **5** brain
6 opportunity

Evaluate, page 27   *Answers will vary.*